Fear of Dying

How to Overcome the Fear of Death in Order to Fully Enjoy Life

by Juri Hansen

Table of Contents

Introduction 1

Chapter 1: The Last Thing You Will Ever Have to Do 7

Chapter 2: Finding Out What You REALLY Fear .. 15

Chapter 3: When Your Fear of Dying Affects Others 23

Chapter 4: Practical Tips to Overcome a Fear of Dying 27

Chapter 5: Why We Don't Know What Is Beyond Death 33

Conclusion 37

Introduction

You've probably heard it dozens of times before, that death is an inevitable part of life. Deep down you know it to be true, and yet you're still haunted by your fear of death. Many of the times you've spent mulling over that inevitable end of the road perhaps overpowered your ability to convince yourself that you must accept that's how it is, and so you might as well get on with life. Maybe you were even convinced by somebody else to accept what's ultimately coming and get on with the business of right now, whether directly through their communication with you or indirectly, through your observation of the way it doesn't seem to bother them.

It's one thing if your curiosity surrounding death breeds questions of the meaning of life, but it's a totally different story if your obstructive views on death constantly plague you to the point where the quality of your daily life suffers. If your thoughts on death are nothing more than a periodic consideration in passing, you can probably quite easily call yourself back to order and not allow the quality of your life to suffer as a result. But if you're living your life at 'half mast' however, and your compromised existence can be directly attributed to your fear of dying, you are going to have to address your fear of death in a bid to enjoy life more.

It's perfectly natural for you to wonder about the point of life, and you may find yourself entertaining a number of different questions stemming from your fear of dying, adding fuel to your compromised-life fire. Often, the people who allow their lives to be compromised by their fear of death find themselves asking questions like "Why are we all here?", most importantly, "Why am I here?" and you may even question the relevance of life-activities such as getting an education, developing a set of skills, and generally taking part in society.

What's the point of everything in between if it's one day all going to come to an end and effectively result in nothingness? Assumedly, your short-term engagements are justified, such as going to work so that you can have the money to do the things you need and want to do (sustain yourself and your loved ones). Beyond that however, is what notoriously stirs up all these questions, ultimately leading to the fear of dying and a subsequent compromised state of existence.

Perhaps your fear of death is more of an immediate one, and you are wary of all the dangers normal life on earth poses. You might be refraining from engaging in anything which is deemed a risk in order to avoid what is often referred to an 'untimely death'.

Whatever form your fear of dying takes, it ultimately comes down to the here-and-now. If your fear of death is hindering you from fully enjoying life, then it's time you dealt with it. This book is designed to show you how to turn your deep-running desire for answers into a catalyst for fully enjoying your life. Your fear of death is going to be exposed for what it really is, which will inevitably help you regain control of exactly what it is that life has to offer you. Read on to discover how to get past your fear of death so that you can enjoy a fuller and more satisfying life.

© Copyright 2015 by Miafn LLC - All rights reserved.

This document is geared towards providing reliable information in regards to the topic and issue covered. The publication is sold with the idea that the publisher is not required to render accounting, officially permitted, or otherwise, qualified services. If advice is necessary, legal or professional, a practiced individual in the profession should be ordered.

- From a Declaration of Principles which was accepted and approved equally by a Committee of the American Bar Association and a Committee of Publishers and Associations.

In no way is it legal to reproduce, duplicate, or transmit any part of this document in either electronic means or in printed format. Recording of this publication is strictly prohibited and any storage of this document is not allowed unless with written permission from the publisher. All rights reserved.

The information provided herein is stated to be truthful and consistent, in that any liability, in terms of inattention or otherwise, by any usage or abuse of any policies, processes, or directions contained within is solely and completely the responsibility of the recipient reader. Under no circumstances will any legal responsibility or blame be held against the publisher for any reparation, damages, or monetary loss due to the information herein, either directly or indirectly.

Respective authors own all copyrights not held by the publisher.

The information herein is offered for informational purposes solely, and is universal as so. The presentation of the information is without contract or any type of guarantee assurance.

The trademarks that are used are without any consent, and the publication of the trademark is without permission or backing by the trademark owner. All trademarks and brands within this book are for clarifying purposes only and are the owned by the owners themselves, not affiliated with this document.

Chapter 1: The Last Thing You Will Ever Have to Do

Keeping in mind that the ultimate goal here is for you to re-capture your zest for life and enjoy a full life, your attitude towards death will have to be shaken up a bit. The idea to overcome your fear of death expressed in this chapter could very well be passed off as "testing the waters." You will be encouraged to complete a quick and easy mental exercise to determine just how deeply your fear of death affects your day-to-day quality of life.

Your day-to-day quality of life is dictated to by the finest of margins, especially in relation to your views on death and just how much of a hold you allow those views to have over you. Everything you do daily ultimately comes down to the decisions you make—if you break your day down into its various moments, you will very quickly realize that your day is indeed made up of a series of decisions. Do you choose to wake up early in the morning so that you can have more time to enjoy your breakfast and prepare for work, or do you prefer to hit the snooze button and enjoy five more minutes of restless sleep? Would you rather rush home after work, only to be stuck in traffic, or would it do you better to sit down for a cup of coffee with a colleague you're fond of and get to know them better while riding out the peak-hour traffic?

These are merely a couple of examples of the thinking you should adopt, which you can implement immediately in an attempt to prune the effects of your negative views on death. Break things down to a level where you want to make the best decision that will help you enjoy the moment more, or the period of time immediately following that moment. If your compromised daily life is as a result of a mild fear of dying, this proactive and loosely calculated way of thinking will do the trick and you'll find yourself enjoying life more and worrying less about what death will bring with it.

Understand that although it is inevitable, death comes stone-last in everyone's life, including yours. Death comes at the very end of it all, no matter how long or short your life will ultimately turn out to be. In the meantime, you have some living to do and until the day of your death comes, get busy living.

Find Daily Motivation to Live Life Fully

If you're reading this book right now, your next thought is probably that getting over your fear of death and living in-the-now proves a lot easier said than done. Otherwise you would have just got on with it, right? Since the aim here is to help you lead a much more enjoyable and fuller life in spite of the fact that you know it's all going to end one day, the ideas communicated will point you in the direction you already want to be going in your life. Regardless of your knowledge of the inevitability of death and perhaps your fear of death, there are certain things in life which you simply make the time and effort to get done. It could be going to work, making sure the kids have everything they need, taking a bath or keeping up with current affairs by watching the news. Why do you do all of those things and why do you keep doing all of those things, even though many aspects of your life are hindered by your fear of dying?

The simple answer is because you feel as if you have to—you feel obliged, whatever the motivation may be. This is where your inherent obligation should be turned into something positive. In a classic case of turning something negative into something positive, procrastination is encouraged when it comes to tackling your fear of death. If you think about it a little deeper, you will agree that the biological arm of science suggests that we all started dying from the day we were born. There is a period in your life (when you're growing up from a toddler right up to adulthood) during which your development as a human being goes in one direction, upwards. As a child, teenager and young-adult, you enjoy or enjoyed having more energy, your body healed quicker from injuries and you recovered easier and quicker from illnesses.

Past a certain threshold however, things seem to be going in the other direction and you find that you have to engage your body and mind more in order to reach the same heights you may have scaled when you were younger. This merely alludes to the fact that we all started dying from the day we drew our first breath and what it means for you is that you are dying as you read this. You may not be suffering from any terminal diseases or ailments and you may not be living in a war zone where a stray bullet could hit you at any time and end it all in an instant.

We are all susceptible to the effects of time and it is essentially what you choose to do with your time that will dictate just how much you enjoy living your life. Again, procrastination is encouraged in this instance and since death comes at the very end—since death is the very last thing you'll ever have to do in your life—

until then, live in the moment and enjoy the life that you currently have.

Now, with the idea that death is the very last thing you'll have to do in mind, evaluate your current situation and look at all the activities you complete in your daily life. You can do this in real time, whenever you're doing something (anything really), or you can plan ahead and take stock of what your typical day is like. In every situation you subsequently find yourself, think of quick ways to make that situation better, even if just by a little bit. For example, if you're slaving away in your office so that you can pay the bills come the end of the month, think of ways to make the best of your situation. Could you perhaps pop on some soft music or add a plant to liven up your environment? Could you perhaps learn how to use a new piece of technology which will make your routine tasks go much quicker and smoother?

This constant evaluation of what you can do to make your immediate situation better should carry over into all aspects of your life. No matter how big or small the situation you find yourself in, the mere process of thinking of ways to make it better (even if by a small fraction) will go a long way in helping you get busy living while you're dying. Implementing those identified deliverables goes even further in nullifying the negative effects that your fear of dying may have on your life.

Finally, keeping in mind that we are all busy dying, including yourself, consider this -- while you were busy dying, from the moment of your birth up until now, were there any moments when you experienced pure joy and completely forgotten about your fear of dying? The answer is invariably "yes" and your focus should then be to shift to trying to recreate those moments while you continue to die. Get that right and your somewhat justified fear of death won't have a chance to influence the quality of your daily life.

Chapter 2: Finding Out What You REALLY Fear

Is it *really* death which you fear?

In this chapter, our focus will shift a little bit away from your fear of death itself. Unless you fear the physical suffering of a painful death, chances are you're not really afraid of death itself—you're probably not really afraid of the ultimate end. Whatever your religious or spiritual beliefs may be, especially concerning what happens when we die, nobody can truly claim to know exactly what it is that happens when the end comes. That mystery is essentially where your fear stems from as people are hard-wired to fear or try to steer clear of the unknown.

As much intrigue as mystery sparks, it can just as easily breed fear and the development of unhealthy levels of uncertainty. Understanding something a little bit more goes a long way to mitigate any undue fears surrounding whatever it is, and it is no different with death. Your focus will now shift to identifying what type of fear you have surrounding death, prior to suggesting solutions you can implement to ensure that fear doesn't hinder the quality of your daily life.

Dealing with Your Literal Fear of Death

As has been established, your fear of death may take a literal form, in that you might be physically afraid of the process of dying. If that is the case, then you undoubtedly find yourself letting life pass you by, and you tend to opt out of a number of activities from which a lot of joy can be extracted.

You would never do something like going sky-diving or anything like that that is considered to be extreme in nature. To that degree, your risk-aversion is probably still very justifiable, in that something like sky-diving is indeed considered to be markedly extreme, even for adrenalin junkies. If you avoid driving at all costs however, or if your fear of death has you abnormally paranoid about security, your health or even something like the durability of the building you're in, dealing with your fear should start with taking a broad look at how death presents itself.

When it is your time, it is your time and in no way can you influence the course of your ultimate destiny. Understand that you are not in control of when your time comes. When someone dies, it's never their own fault, even if the circumstances surrounding their death suggest so. This applies to suicides too -- nobody just wakes up one day and thinks suicide is a good idea, out of the blue. Their suicide is likely forced upon them by circumstances, when life become too much to bear.

If your fear of dying takes the form of an inhibited state of being as a result of being wary of all the dangers of this world, you simply have to free yourself from your inhibitions by accepting the fact that death comes when it is time for it to come. That's exactly the reason why a lot of deaths are unexplainable, leaving everybody in utter shock as to how this could possibly have happened. You might hear of the healthiest gym-rat-cum-health-nut suddenly passing away as a result of a short illness, or even the most careful of drivers falling victim to a fatal car accident. On the other side of the coin, you can have the highest risk-taking adrenalin junkies living through all their daring escapades to a ripe old age.

It is not suggested that you do away with all self-awareness and abandon your responsibilities, but think of it this way—if it's your time, it's your time, and if it's not yet your time, nothing will happen to you. With that in mind, there is a simple exercise you can do in order to move away from your fear of dying compromising the quality of your life, while not crossing the risk-threshold to operate at blatantly dangerous levels.

Exercise: When faced with a situation that requires you take a risk of some sort, there is a great way to analyze whether you should take that risk or not. Very simply put, if you stand to gain more from taking that risk than what you have to lose, it's probably a risk worth-taking. If you have more to lose than you have to gain, then you can write it off as taking a good decision not to put yourself in any compromising situation. Make a game of it and train yourself in this way to always make the right decision.

Mistakes are an inevitable part of the process, but embrace your mistakes as learning curves. Don't let your learning curves present themselves to you in the form of epic mistakes from which it would be very hard to recover.

As you go along, you will find that perhaps your fear of death was a little bit overstated and that instead of life offering nothing but fatal hazards at every corner, it has a lot more enjoyment to offer you.

Finding out What You Really Fear

Again, if you analyze your fear of dying with a bit more of a trained mind, you are likely to discover that it is not death itself which you fear, but rather the dynamics surrounding it. That said, those dynamics surrounding death require some insight in order for you to take back control of the way in which you live and consequently how you enjoy your life.

With regards to your fear, death can be likened to a war-zone. If you turn on the news on TV and hear about a war going on in a specified location, you might incorrectly refer to that place as a dangerous place. For example in Libya, Iraq, Pakistan and parts of Nigeria, wars of some sort are reported to be taking place in recent times. You might loosely refer to those regions as dangerous places, but a country in its capacity as a geographic location cannot be dangerous on its own, unless it is riddled with natural disasters, surface hazards and the like. What makes those places dangerous are the people in arms fighting the wars. To expand on the analogy further, the guns that the soldiers carry do not pose any danger by themselves. It is the people who carry those weapons and use them for destructive purposes.

In the same way as a war-torn country or region is not dangerous by itself, death poses no direct threat to you and should therefore not be feared directly. It is what death symbolizes which is probably the root cause for your concern. Death symbolizes the end of your life as you know it—the only way you know it—

and everything surrounding death is where you should look to find inspiration for the full enjoyment of your life.

Putting aside all precompiled and previously inspired religious or spiritual beliefs, imagine for a second that you are dead—you died yesterday, and as part of the post-death process, you are asked to compile a list of all the regrets you have. Do you fear that your tombstone will have nothing more than a short description of who you were because of your distinct lack of significant accomplishments in your life? Are you perhaps afraid that there won't be enough money left to give you a proper send-off? Do you perhaps wish you'd mended a broken relationship with someone once dear to you? Do you wish you'd felt what it feels like to swim with sharks, or learned to play an instrument? Whatever it is, that is essentially what fuels your fear of death and that is essentially what hinders you from fully enjoying life.

Be specific and detailed about what your regrets might be, should it all come to an end, as it inevitably will. Once you have a clear picture of all the regrets you might have when the end comes, rectify that through your daily actions. Live your daily life in such a way that if death came at any time, you would have been absolutely fine with it. In the process, you will open up the door into a whole new world of possibilities and there will be no time and space for the negative effects of the fear of death to take effect.

Chapter 3: When Your Fear of Dying Affects Others

When your fear of death is not limited to your own specific life, it can have a significant effect on your loved-ones. It's only natural to worry about the safety and well-being of those you love, but you can really stunt the development of your family members, such as your children, if you wrap them in cotton wool in a genuine attempt to shield them from the dangers of this world. Furthermore, this goes back to the stunted quality of your own life as you spend less of your time doing the things you love doing and more of it worrying about the safety of your loved-ones.

In this case, a balance between the right amount of concern and avoiding being over-protective is the ultimate goal and it can be achieved via a simple altering of your mindset.

Pretty much the same approach to dealing with your own fear of death applies, in that you should trust in the fact that your loved-ones possess an inherent survival instinct, which is reinforced by that inevitable fact that death comes only when it is destined to. By no means is it suggested that you should stop worrying altogether or that you should abandon your responsibilities. What you should do is to simply let your loved-ones be, and perhaps you can discuss your concerns with them. Communication solves a lot of problems and you might find that they have the same concerns as you do, in which case they will make it much easier for you to deal with your fear.

Formulate a checking-in structure, where you communicate with each other and let each other know that all's well. This is the best way to pave the way for your focus to shift back to the important business at hand, which is to find a way to extract more enjoyment out of living your life, instead of constantly worrying about death.

Get in touch with your loved-ones now and initiate the discussed checking-in campaign.

Chapter 4: Practical Tips to Overcome a Fear of Dying

Chapters 1 through 3 covered some specific ways in which you can overcome your fear of death in order to enjoy a full life. The detailed approach of understanding the dynamics surrounding death is essential to your eventual success at alleviating or completely overcoming your fear, but there are a few practical, more instant ways you can initiate the process of living your life to the fullest, in-spite of your fears.

1. **Look for any excuse to celebrate anything life has to offer:** Go beyond the usual holidays, birthdays, etc. People who enjoy their lives fully don't need a special occasion to celebrate. Every day can be a celebration.

2. **Engage in spirituality, rituals, religion, or create new traditions**: Religion and spiritual endeavors can offer you instant direction as to exactly what to do in the moment to make the best of it. Rituals or traditions you create yourself can also do the trick and give you a great starting point for discovering new ways of making the most of the time you have available.

3. **Treat yourself like royalty:** Live well and don't make do with half-measures. If the best of what life has to offer was not reserved for you, then who else is it reserved for and what makes them so special? Treat yourself like royalty and others will at least ask themselves why they're not treating you like royalty as well.

4. **Plan for your inevitable passing:** Plan for your death by either telling loved ones how you want to depart this earth or by taking out life cover, funeral cover, etc. Write a will or plan in any other way—it's very therapeutic and will go a long way in addressing your fears of dying, head-on.

5. **Take a field trip that somewhere out of your comfort zone:** Either visit something like an old age home, a hospital, or have a talk with someone who is nearer to their death than you are. Discretion will be required, obviously, and you should be subtle about it. Ask an older person if they're afraid to die and, if so, why. If they answer "no", sit up and take note—you will probably come away with a wealth of knowledge and wisdom that will help you deal with your own fear.

6. **Take good care of yourself:** Enjoying life while "waiting" for your death depends solely upon your health. Take good care of yourself in every way possible so that you are healthy enough to engage in all the activities you suspect will add some more joy to your life.

7. **Be curious and strive to reward your curiosity:** Explore your curiosity and see where it takes you. There are few better feelings in the world than getting a satisfactory answer to a question that has been eating you up all along. Curiosity also leads to discovery and you could quite easily discover some great new ways to overcome your fears of dying.

8. **Communicate:** Talk to others. They might shine a light on a different perspective, and perhaps they're even going through the same challenges you are. A problem shared is a problem halved, so get talking.

9. **Make plans as if you're going to live forever:** You don't quite know exactly how long you're going to live, so make plans as if you're going to live forever. You might live for a very, very long time and find yourself with way more time to kill than you anticipated. The ensuing emptiness can only be replaced by enjoyment and fulfillment, if you have plans in place to spend that time more constructively.

10. **Put your best foot forward:** This is probably one of the best ways to ensure you enjoy your life fully. Whether it's dressing up to the nines or competing in a friendly competition, put your best foot forward, give your best and you'll never have to worry about living life at half-mast.

11. **Explore life (embracing disappointments and mistakes along the way):** Life is there for the taking. Don't limit yourself to what status quo requires. Some gems are waiting to be uncovered if you simply take the time to look.

12. **Create priorities and goals:** Don't stop prioritizing goals, even if they appear to be too far away. Again, you don't know how long you're ultimately going to live and you don't want to find yourself with more time to kill than things to do.

13. **Make a bucket list:** Create a list of 101 things to do before you die, and start doing them. Your list is personal and it can definitely evolve over time. Make a point to also include a few items that you would consider to be daring.

14. **Help others and help improve the world:** Getting a smile of gratitude from helping someone in real need probably has no equal by way of inducing a feeling of real satisfaction and accomplishment. See if you can help somebody, in whatever small way possible, and make a habit of it.

15. **Start each new day on a clean slate:** Everyday signifies the opportunity to start afresh—grab that opportunity with both hands and you'll be well on your way to replacing your fear of death with a full life of joy and happiness.

Chapter 5: Why We Don't Know What Is Beyond Death

As a typical expression of human nature, while you can try and implement everything you learned about curbing your fear of death to fully enjoy life, you can still periodically have those fears re-surface all over again. If this happens, take refuge in the fact that there is a reason why we don't know for sure what happens when we die. Different religions have different explanations, so it would be impossible to guess the right one, if any, between all of their explanations.

The reason we don't know what happens for sure when we die is that if you knew, you would essentially have nothing to live for. Your life would be nothing more than a transitional period, which it is, but because of the fact that we don't know when, how and why death exists, we can spend less time worrying about death itself and rather focus on our borrowed time on earth.

In particular, if death signifies the beginning of something which is far greater than what life currently has to offer, and you knew that for sure, you would probably live your life and try to enjoy each moment in any case. If death alternatively signified the beginning of a less-than-ideal progression, you would still live your life to the fullest, knowing that what lies ahead isn't something you're looking forward to.

Either way, whatever death ultimately brings, you are in control of the life you have right now and it's up to you to make a choice between either making it as pleasant as possible or succumbing to your fear of death and its impingement on the quality of your life.

Conclusion

Overcoming the fear of dying in order to fully enjoy life starts with understanding the dynamics surrounding death. Is it really the process of dying you're afraid of, which is ultimately keeping you from enjoying each day of your life? Or are you afraid of what legacy you will leave behind when the end inevitably comes?

If you are afraid of the literal process itself, conduct some on-the-go risk analysis of possible situations you might face, where feasible of course. If you stand to gain more than you stand to lose, go for it, but if you stand to lose more than you stand to gain, avoiding that risk is justifiable. However, be careful not to let that re-ignite your fears of death, and the subsequent hindrance of the quality of your current existence.

Virtually the same approach applies to fears of death concerning loved-ones—let them be, and communicate your concerns with them, with the aim of devising an on-going communication platform through which you can keep an eye on each other, in a healthy way.

If you discover that your fear of death isn't exactly a fear of the literal process of death, explore the different possible sources of this fear that inhibits you from living out your life fully. It almost invariably goes back to the legacy you will leave behind, if only for your own satisfaction. Un-rewarded curiosity can be the worst feeling to deal with and you have the chance to rectify that with the dawn of each day, while you're still alive.

If you require some instant, practical measures to implement in a bid to curb your fear of death and fully enjoy your life, you can easily draw on the 15 steps suggested in Chapter 4. Practice them until they become second nature to you.

Remember that death is inevitable, whether you choose to make the most of the time you have between then and now or otherwise, the choice ultimately lies with you. Choose wisely!

Finally, I'd like to thank you for purchasing this book! If you found it helpful, I'd greatly appreciate it if you'd take a moment to leave a review on Amazon. Thank you!

Printed in Great Britain
by Amazon